Aaron Betsky

UNSTUDIO

The Floating Space

TASCHEN

HONG KONG KÖLN LONDON LOS ANGELES MADRID PARIS TOKYO

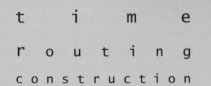

t i m e

r o u t i n g

c o n s t r u c t i o n

Photo page 2 ▸ Ben van Berkel on site
Illustration page 3 ▸ Diagram of the Living
Tomorrow Pavilion
Illustration page 4 ▸ Computer graphics for the
Möbius House

© 2007 TASCHEN GmbH
Hohenzollernring 53, D-50672 Köln
www.taschen.com

Editor ▸ Peter Gössel, Bremen
Design and layout ▸ Gössel und Partner, Bremen
Project management ▸ Katrin Schumann, Eike
Meyer, Bremen
Text edited by ▸ Sally Schreiber for
Zoratti studio editoriale

Printed in Germany
ISBN: 978-3-8228-4538-7

To stay informed about upcoming TASCHEN
titles, please request our magazine at
www.taschen.com/magazine or write to
TASCHEN America, 6671 Sunset Boulevard,
Suite 1508, USA-Los Angeles, CA 90028,
contact-us@taschen.com, Fax: +1-323-463.4442.
We will be happy to send you a free copy of our
magazine which is filled with information about
all of our books.

Content

Introduction

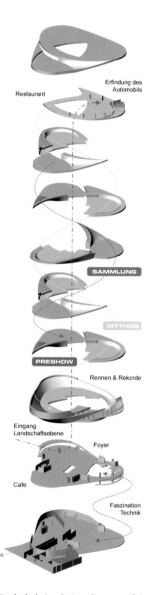

Restaurant

Erfindung des
Automobils

SAMMLUNG

MYTHOS

PRESHOW

Rennen & Rekorde

Eingang
Landschaftsebene

Foyer

Cafe

Faszination
Technik

Exploded circulation diagram of the Mercedes-Benz Museum, showing two intertwining routes

Opposite page:
Mercedes-Benz Museum, Stuttgart, Germany, 2001–2006
View from entrance plaza

The position of architecture in the early 21st century is controversial and thus the form of buildings that aspire to convey meaning is often convoluted. If a building is to succeed it must be a monster: something unknowable, animal, and yet vaguely familiar, as if it had risen out of our deepest unconscious. It must be bigger and stranger than we are, and yet a mirror of our hopes and fears. This is the position that has been maintained by Ben van Berkel, Caroline Bos and their firm—now known as UNStudio—for the last fifteen years. In an era in which investment in an autonomous monumental object would seem like financial, moral and intellectual folly, these architects have been making the argument for strong, folded, warped and inverted forms as a condenser of economic resources as well as of concrete. They see buildings as place-holders as well as containers of spatial labyrinths, and as iconic forms as well as unknowable shapes. They argue that the unified, but highly complex, assertion of a building can give a solid representation and perhaps even narrative meaning to the otherwise invisible and incomprehensible forces that shape our daily lives. As such, they are architects in the old-fashioned heroic mode, however strange their buildings might appear. They are not slayers, but makers of dragons.

To create these buildings, van Berkel and Bos have relied on computer and construction technology that allows their shapes to present complex phenomena rising beyond the pure presentation of form, function or context. Their work has tended equally toward the development of autonomous effects as toward the production of solitary, constructed forms; toward continuous space or surface as much as toward the making of a coherent, hierarchical representation of a single idea about the contents of a building. UNStudio's buildings, in other words, do not show us how, why or where they were made, nor do they tell us what they are good for. Instead, they try to add something that is not strictly necessary to the project of housing a particular individual, corporation or institution. What they add is architecture, and that peculiar quality allows us to understand the place made as something different from and more than the sum of all of its parts.

Thus the Mercedes-Benz Museum, undoubtedly their most significant work to date, not only provides all of the space needed to display the company's collections but also efficiently moves people through the exhibits. However this space is not in the form of discreet galleries, but rather two intertwined, continuous ramps which allow visitors to pursue two different narrative routes through the history of the automobile—or to construct a hybrid history of their own.

The building's exterior reflects this complex organization, yet unifies it into a form that is not quite comprehensible. This shape seems appropriate to its setting, but in a manner that we cannot rationalize. There are hints of the Daimler's corporate logo in the whole design, but they are never made explicit. Taken as a whole, this is a project of giving shape and thus a unified presence in a particular place to an abstract corporate entity that, over the last century, has produced a series of automobiles of considerable note and distinction. The contribution of the architecture is to let us

City of the Captive Globe by Rem Koolhaas and Madelon Vriesendorp, 1972

experience what is otherwise a vague character as a coherent and logical whole and to mine that history for a kind of beauty beyond the consumer objects that Mercedes-Benz produces.

As such, the work of UNStudio is not critical, but neither does it merely stand in the service of the client. It tries to make the argument for architecture as something that adds a particular quality of image, space and form by which we can establish our own relationship to, and maintain our autonomy against, that which we are experiencing. In the end, the autonomous architecture UNStudio produces is we ourselves as we experience the work and through it try to make sense of our world.

The roots for this approach go back to the peculiar situation of architecture in the late 1970s and early 1980s, and in particular to London's Architectural Association (AA), where van Berkel and Bos met in the 1980s. At this time architecture seemed to be coming close to dying. In a period of prolonged economic recession and after the certainties of a technologically driven economy and culture seemed to have been completely dissipated by their failure to enhance people's lives or meet any of the other lofty postwar goals, architects began to doubt that they had anything they could provide in terms of certain and efficient housing. The grids, the function-driven forms and structural bravura of high modernism had been played out and found to be non-human. While some architects turned back to the period before modernism to take solace in historical styles, and others mined the most abstract aspects of architecture in what Michel Foucault called "an archaeology of knowledge," (which is to say, an investigation of the origins and structures of patterns or cognition and ordering), a small group of architects and thinkers at the AA began unfolding and elaborating existing physical reality to discover the potential for new forms, organizational patterns and meaning.

Led by Rem Koolhaas, Elia Zenghelis, Bernard Tschumi and Daniel Libeskind, this diverse group of designers inspired a whole generation of architects to raise architecture beyond function, context, or form. Their work had a mythological quality to it, as it

Model from the exhibition *Application &*
Implication in Grenoble, 1993

imagined another world that was neither utopian nor dystopian, but definitely beyond reality as it could be experienced. Though their visions might not have been buildable, the effect of their drawings was to invent a whole series of new forms and techniques that proved highly useful for younger designers. Their efforts quickly became known as "deconstructivism," especially after the 1992 exhibition at New York's Museum of Modern Art (MoMA) of that name.

It was this new language of architecture that van Berkel and Bos picked up in London. It consisted of fragments, as the whole was something theoreticians at the time thought represented an impossible certitude. Its geometry was angular and open-ended for similar reasons, though it also resembled the art and fashion of the period. Prows, skewed pentagrams, elongated rectangles, calligraphic swirls, and intersecting piles of lines were the most common elements one could find in this stew of purposefully abstract and unfinished forms.

Behind these images was a set of theories, or at least shared attitudes and beliefs. The notion that architecture had to rebuild itself out of the detritus of a failed construction—whether that of the city, of modernist boxes, or of the educational system in which these forms were being generated—was the most predominant sentiment. There was also a strong realization that architecture was a kind of language, a way to represent and communicate social, economic and physical structures. The realization that autonomy was a fiction, whether in the case of the human body, the building or philosophies behind them, became almost universal in more design-oriented architecture schools such as the AA.

The techniques architects learned to create buildings out of these ideas were less those of the scientists their elders had aspired to be, and more those of the hunters and gatherers, the surfers and the scavengers that were becoming more and more part of the urban scene. As corporate raiders replaced institutionalized corporations, as guerillas defeated standing armies, as clothes and design consisted more and more of bits and pieces borrowed from exotic cultures, as knowledge increasingly became

9

**Hamseweg housing and offices, Amersfoort,
The Netherlands, 1991**

something one gathered from a wide variety of sources that would soon include the Internet, and as the last certainties of class, race, nation and family were wiped away by the corrosive logic of late capitalism, it indeed made sense to trace these uncertain movements in the act of assembling whatever structure might house these very forces of instability.

While some architects believed that this state of flux could only be answered by the fluid dynamics of computer-aided design, or that to invest time and money in the making of solid structures was a vain activity, others began searching for ways in which one could produce moments of stillness, anchors in an unstable world, moments of sense and sensuality, and forms that would allow one to understand this almost incomprehensible world. I believe that van Berkel and Bos have been searching for such moments of solidity ever since. Their work is a phoenix that rises from the ashes of late modernism, and belongs to a family of such resurgent forms that have reinvigorated architecture.

Their first works, produced when they returned to their native Netherlands in the late 1980s, were collages. They masked what were essentially compact boxes behind facades that consisted of various materials, geometries and planes all coming together to make a façade that had a plastic quality. It was as if the final building wore a mask of incompletion. Such was certainly the case in the small office building they designed in the city of Amersfoort. Very quickly, however, more unified forms began to appear. The Karbouw Offices of 1993 and the Electrical Substation of the following year, both in Amersfoort, are shaped and even deformed buildings. Though their skins are still collages, they also take on a sculptural shape. At the time, the making of such a self-confident object sitting in the landscape, however much its form would not refer to historical types and might be "unreadable," was a bold move. The architects were asserting their belief in the autonomous object. At the time, they insisted that they wanted to create an architecture "between the blob and box." They adapted computer-design tools and were sympathetic to the notion that this computational device would result in different kinds of images and forms that were optimized around points of attraction, rather than spread out evenly around site, program and structure. Yet they also were interested in the building as condenser of a complex amount of activity into a compact shape.

The solution to the tension between the logic of how the building was designed and the architects' desire to make something that would take its place in the physical environment was a strategy they developed in the late 1990s. They called it "deep planning." Harking back to techniques developed by Dutch urban planners in the 1920s, and rediscovered by Rem Koolhaas in the early 1990s, deep planning used the computer as a tool for collecting and assimilating diverse data on everything from zoning ordinances and building codes to usage patterns, from material strength to the most efficient constellation of programmatic elements. That same computer could then create relationships among these diverse data. The complexity and instability of a world reduced to zeros and ones could also be tamed by computer formulas. The architect could then shape these abstract relationships into coherent form.

As UNStudio—the name van Berkel and Bos had by then given to their office—began to obtain more and more complex commissions, this form of organization proved useful in allowing the designers to come up with forms that did not mimic the typological variations that were the usual solution to such situations. Thus a shopping mall and housing combination could become a collection of sharply angular fragments that worked together to complete the urban fabric of Amsterdam (De Kolk, 1996). Most successfully, an intermodal transit hub in the city of Arnhem could become a knot of concrete twisting its way out of a parking garage into the central elements of the train and bus stations, spreading out to encompass ancillary programs, and rising up into two office towers that both optimize the intense investment at this one spot and signal the development to the surrounding city.

The other effect of UNStudio's approach was to unearth forces that are latent or hidden in our world and turn them into highly recognizable forms. The first and most famous example of this approach was their design for the Erasmus Bridge in Rotterdam of 1996. Though its form was related to advances in thinking in structural theory that were prevalent at the time, it was especially the way in which the asymmetrical curve of the roadway, supported by its singular splayed pylon, unfolded out of the urban landscape that made the bridge such a natural and yet startling addition to the skyline and urban landscape. "The Swan," as the bridge came to be called by the local population, did not just assert itself as a symbol of the new Rotterdam, but it also unfolded that reality with a great deal of ease, thereby turning a road into a three-dimensional shape and, as it rose, making room for places of gathering such as a large café.

The subsequent tunnels, bridges and electrical stations that have formed a continual bass beat to UNStudio's lyrical moments of formal expression all share this quality of being rooted in both the logic of the physical landscape and acting as nodal points in an urban infrastructure. Almost by default, van Berkel and Bos had found an

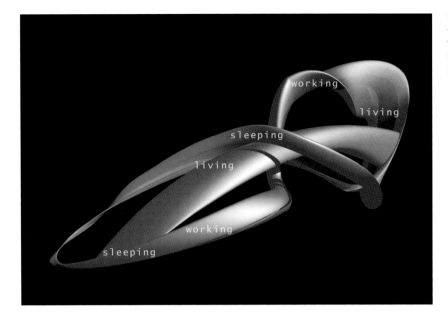

arena in which the making of distinctive and sculptural form is a natural response to the situation. After all, in a world marked more and more by the incessant movement of people, goods and data, what remains is the infrastructure that makes all of this motion possible. That fluidity is also mirrored in the manner in which modern technology can trace and optimize functional and material relationships. The result is fluid form, which the architect then has to manipulate so that it shows motion in a manner that reflects how the infrastructure is made, and allows it to come out of its site with a natural ease. The idea of architecture as an unfolding of reality, the use of collage, the sculpting of form out of a collaged unfolding, and the techniques of deep planning all came together in this set of forms.

At the same time van Berkel and Bos became interested in snipping their buildings off from these flowing forms. Their image for this became the Möbius strip. To van Berkel and Bos this endless form symbolized the ways in which continuous flows, when isolated in a given situation, could develop a singular logic. They found the perfect means to illustrate this in their Möbius House of 1998. There the almost literal translation of the endless strip became a way of organizing the diurnal rhythms by which the owners ritualized the complexity of their daily lives. Van Berkel and Bos illustrated the related Klein Bottle diagram even more literally in their design of a tea service for Alessi in 2002. But more important than these realized representations was the notion that what in the infrastructural projects appeared as ceaseless and borderless flows that crystallized into architecture could actually be isolated and made into autonomous structures. This self-sufficient approach, in which flows pooled into walls that flowed into floors that folded up into stairs or balustrades, all of the pieces interlocking in space, began to inform more and more of their designs. The continuous surface, which was then gaining popularity among architects around the world, made its appearance in several of their projects (most notably the Neutron Magnetic Resonance Facility at the University of Utrecht, also of 2002) as a way of folding the flows back on themselves.

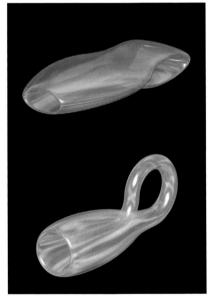

Klein Bottle
A mathematical model of a form that wraps around itself.

While the forms shifted, flowed and returned back to themselves, however, they did not remain the same. They changed geometry and shape, of course, but van Berkel and Bos began to notice that they also changed character. The theory they found that helped them explain this was that of the "manimal." This mythological creature halfway between a human being and fauna had perhaps escaped from the strange landscapes that had unfurled around them at the AA, but also was the result of the imagery released by "morphing" software at the beginning of the 1990s. To van Berkel and Bos, the manimal was an unstable form that had all the qualities of humanity that we expect to find in architecture, in that it mimics our bodies, but that also is a strange thing, an alien—as any building is bound to be something we cannot quite comprehend because it is not an exact mirror of our individual corporeal existence. Rather than experience this simple and very old truth in architecture as a tension that had to be solved by deciding either for the alien being or human representation, or that could be buried underneath some manner of complex or monumental form, they argued for this hybrid, animate character as the very essence of architecture. To be able to make something that simultaneously shared the qualities of familiarity and strangeness, reflection and alienation, organic coherence and constructed artifice became their architectural goal.

One logical extension of this argument was that architecture should become an effect operating on the mere appearance of a building so that it would remain unstable and unknowable. A series of experiments at the beginning of the new millennium led them to façade treatments in which pure light and color made it impossible to decide the building's underlying reality. It was as if the architects had decided that it was not the mass or the space of the building that needed their attention, but the way in which it appeared. Truth be told, the result was in many ways more immediate and easy to grasp than that of their more complex designs. In projects such as the La Defense office building of 2002 or the department store in Seoul two years later one can find an architecture of pure phenomena that was no longer a crystal forged out of flows, but a

Summer of Love Exhibition, Schirn Kunsthalle, Frankfurt am Main, Germany, 2005

prism through which flows passed, creating a moment of beauty, variety and coherence that one could not grasp, but that occurs over and over again.

This focus on visual effects, however, has not become the mainstay of what UNStudio produces. The firm continues to oscillate between boxes and blobs. The internal coherence for these complex forms comes out of deep planning, while the designers have become better and better at combining these separate elements of a building into seamless, continuous collages whose fragmentary nature has given way to a monumental presence. While some projects, such as the housing in Almere of 2001, or the recently completed Theater Agora in Lelystad, exhibit more of the quality of stacked boxes that create a continual space in between their discreet forms, other projects are more fluid. From the Ponte Parodi project, won in competition in 2002, but only just entering the construction phase, to their proposal for a mixed-use complex on London's South Side, the snaking, sinuous shapes the computer can produce remain a central part of UNStudio's formal repertoire. Nor is it a question of evolving from one to the other: their recent Tea House on Bunker (2006) is as aggressive a collection of angular shards as anything they have ever designed.

Van Berkel and Bos justify these hybrid forms with the argument of hybridity itself. They are not interested in making finished, static shapes, as they believe that such objects would not be adequate to the complexities of modern life. Nor are they of the belief that architecture will someday soon dissolve into the organic flow of data, as they think this will leave us without the anchors we need to be able to survive in that fluid

Holiday Home Exhibition, Institute for Contempory Art, Philadelphia, USA, 2006

reality. Instead, they seek to make shapes that are both fluid and solid. As such, they both represent our modern world and thus are profoundly modernist in the belief that this is the task of all art and architecture, and offer a memory of something beyond what we can experience in the here and now. The latter aspect of the elusive, but vaguely familiar, solid and mute presence in the human landscape becomes their answer to the question what the task of architecture might be beyond the representation of all that goes into the act and fact of building.

This is not to say that all their buildings look like each other or are all either blob-like or collections of shards, or a combination thereof. In fact, UNStudio seems to make it a point to now and then produce a work that is purposefully odd or not what one might expect from them, such as the Het Valkhof Museum of 1999, the small church they designed in 2000 in Hilversum, or the more recent Hotel Castell of 2004. All these are more restrained, box-like forms that display subtler deformations than most of the other work. They are, perhaps for that reason, among the most elegant structures they have designed thus far. It is as if the architects want to make it a point to show that they have not developed a style, though they do have a mode of working. Instead, they have created an approach to architecture that they see as a rigorous response to a given situation. This answer also addresses the universal conditions under which they and we all operate. They believe it focuses the use of material and the enclosure of form in a more or less optimized fashion that the architect is free to manipulate towards a free representation of something unknowable.

UNStudio itself is meant to reflect this hybrid nature and the desire to bring deep knowledge to bear on three-dimensional representation. Van Berkel and Bos see the firm not as a traditional architecture office, but as a loose cooperative of highly trained professionals who come together around specific projects. Van Berkel, trained as an architect, and Bos, an art historian, are at the core of this coalition, and they have surrounded themselves with a more or less stable collection of designers who have enough institutional memory to be able to carry out the task of getting buildings built with a high degree of efficiency. When necessary or when they desire, however, they reach beyond this office to work together with other designers, as they did in the 2003 competition for Ground Zero. They also see their work as emerging from collaboration with structural engineers and other experts, and extending beyond the making of buildings to writing, creating art, and the design of objects of use. Their work's hybrid coherence is the point, not its place within a discipline or a profession.

For all this complex positioning of architecture at the beginning of this millennium, what really distinguishes van Berkel and Bos' work is a particular character it has in and of itself. Out of deep planning and the unfolding of existing reality, in a world of flows, autonomous and hybrid, the work of UNStudio has amassed a quality that is not just ephemeral, but that is recognizable. There are the elongated, stretched curves, the way these usually concrete forms are attached to more orthogonal, but thinly stretched elements out of steel or some other more brittle material. There are the folded and layered facades. There is the delight in the fractured rectangle or box, itself a three-dimensional version of the collage. There are the prow and the bow, the bulge and the flip—all elements of what is by now a large body of work that one can recognize as the product of a single set of designers. Above all else, there is the way in which all these elements, which otherwise might be just the tricks of architectural stylists, cohere into

Bauhaus Archive Expansion (Competition), Berlin, Germany, 2006

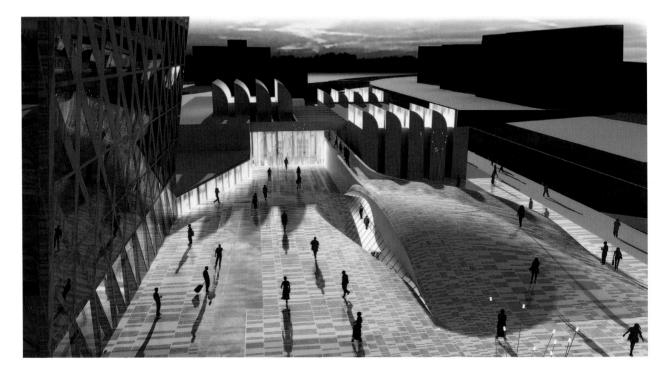

**Arnhem Central Station Project,
The Netherlands, 1996–2008**

forms that somehow give shape to the institutions they house. In so doing, these forms are not just representations of the traditional elements out of which buildings are made, nor are they images of the company, bureaucracy or individual who commissioned them. Moreover, they are also not just the willful expressions of the stylistic preferences of the designers. Instead, they are things in and of themselves. They come out of forces that are human, but they are not themselves of that sort. They have a strong and undeniable presence, but they do not impose themselves solely as dead things in our world. They seem to have risen out of that world, to breathe its air and to flow out of its forces, and they seem to surmount it with a manner of holding place on the outside and space within them that is wholly proper to what they are. It is this enigmatic quality that cloaks the mute forms of building with the elusive and allusive power of architecture.

1989–1993 ▸ Electrical Substation
Amersfoort, The Netherlands

Opposite page:
View from northeast

Three of van Berkel and Bos' earliest designs are in the Dutch provincial town of Amersfoort. To the quaint collection of medieval structures that make up the town's core they have added three buildings that effect the transition to the more recent suburban landscape that surrounds every old town in Europe. Designed as collages of materials that come together to create abstract shapes, they give the new the dignity as well as the complexity time has bequeathed the older buildings.

The substation is, like all such structures, essentially a thin covering over equipment that remains completely anonymous and invisible. The only people who ever use the building are maintenance and control personnel. Thus there are no windows, and there is no need for anything indicating or responding to a human scale, and no differentiation between interior spaces.

Van Berkel and Bos chose to accommodate the mass to its site, between one of the country's busiest railroad lines and a small park behind Amersfoort's City Hall, by breaking it apart into two separate volumes. The darker half, which faces the semi-industrial landscape of the railroad tracks and the warehouses beyond them (which have since been redeveloped), is clad in black basalt plates. The southern section acts as a park structure. Clad in aluminum panels, it is tilted at a slight angle to increase the sense of being lighter and more abstract. In this way the back connects the structure to the ground and the mechanical world, while what might appear as the front is part of the fanciful world of trees—or of the wedding parties that sometimes drift over from City Hall to have their pictures taken against the abstract backdrop of the metal facade.

Van Berkel and Bos subdivided the panels on both sides with a wooden grid that has by now weathered to a grey somewhere between the basalt and aluminum in tone and color. The sides of the two loading bays, lifted slightly off the ground, are clad in the same material, as is the side of the door through which workers enter the structure. The aluminum also continues around the north side of the building to enclose the loading area, causing the whole composition to click into place. One small eyebrow window is the only other differentiating element in what appears at first to be a simple and monolithic block that turns out to be a complex three-dimensional composition monumentalizing the usually invisible infrastructure by means of an aesthetic object hovering between building and sculpture.

Entrance and loading dock

1990–1992 ▸ Karbouw Offices
Amersfoort, The Netherlands

Opposite page:
Entrance with offices above

Right:
Rear façade

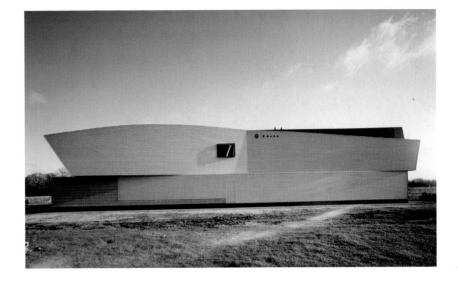

Office interiors

Sited in an anonymous industrial estate in the town of Amersfoort, this modest office and warehouse structure designed for a local builder (the contractor on the firm's other two projects in that city) is a billboard for thoughtful construction as much as it is an efficient container.

The building's two functions are expressed in the two different dominant materials used for base and superstructure. The poured-in-place concrete base is clad in red brick, while the second floor, which contains the offices, is sheathed in corrugated metal plates. The two floors shift away from each other, and that angle gains emphasis from the placement of the entrance door under the corner of the offices where it hangs out over the base. The corrugation acts as a cowl that wraps the glass-fronted offices, while on the building's rear it folds, curves and angles as if it was made out of cloth. Thus the architects make clear that the simple base is a solid object containing bare space and warehoused materials, while the upper floor is a free element whose cladding emphasizes the particularities of the site, the function and the design. The architects pin this composition down with a collection of small elements: a band of darker brick at the building's base, a glass window that pops out of the rear, a glass-enclosed stair hall connecting the two floors and porthole windows that bring light into the rear offices. Inside, the angles are visible and continue into the walls, sheering away part of the cladding to reveal the building's construction. The deliberate play of forms and materials makes us aware of how buildings are made.

1990–1996 ▸ Erasmus Bridge
Rotterdam, The Netherlands

Plan in urban context

Night view from east

The locals call it "the Swan" or "the Harp" and it is a favored location for music videos and television commercials. It has also become the new symbol for Rotterdam, Europe's largest port and the city that is transforming into a multicultural center around the mouth of the Maas. The bridge that has become the city's most visible icon is an almost 460-ft.-high, 2,625-ft.-long span painted a light blue color and named after Rotterdam's most famous resident, Erasmus.

The Erasmus Bridge connects the city's business core to a former inner-city harbor the municipality has been developing into an office and residential quarter since the early 1980s. The two-lane bridge also brings together the white collar and white North of the city with its blue collar and increasingly ethnically diverse South. The city clearly wanted a symbol of what it wanted to become when it selected van Berkel and Bos to design the bridge in 1989.

Van Berkel had worked briefly for Santiago Calatrava, and the bridge picks up where that Spanish wizard of infrastructure left off. The arched roadway hangs from a single, splayed pylon tied back to the southern shore with a single cable. It passes underneath this support to emerge into a 930-ft. free span. To the south of the support, the bridge can open to allow larger ships to pass. Van Berkel and Bos worked with the Rotterdam City Engineer's Office to shave and shape the main structural elements so that they will appear as thin, tall and taut as possible. They also made the bridge into more than just an engineering feat by molding every aspect with the same sculptural care. The bridge starts as roadways, cycle lanes and pedestrian paths unfold themselves from the city's infrastructure. These disparate elements then turn from mere horizontal planes into three-dimensional concrete and steel shapes that then meld and subside into the

Opposite page:
Night view from north

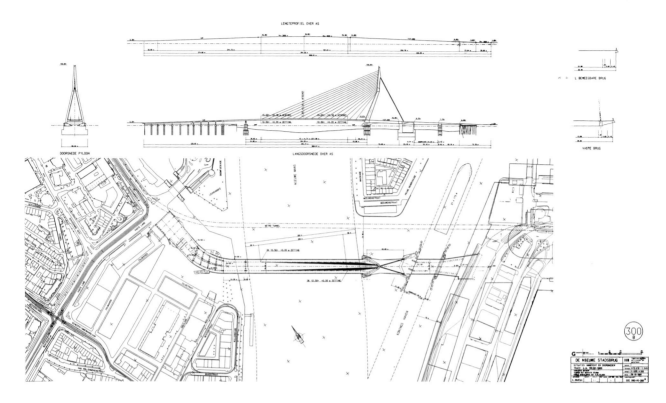

LENGTEPROFIEL OVER AS

DOORSNEDE PYLOON

LANGSDOORSNEDE OVER AS

L BEWEEGBARE BRUG

VASTE BRUG

Plan and sections in urban context

streamlined bridge across the water. Along the way they each become compositions in their own right, giving the passerby a sense of the city abstracting itself into compact volumes that allow for the great leap across the water.

It is the skill with which the bridge unwraps itself from the city to become a soaring abstract object that gives this structure its particular power. In recent years, the firm has continued its work on the site by adding an embarkation station for the local sightseeing company and a market square next to the northern touch-down point, as well as a sizeable bar tucked underneath the span. Combining a sense of the excitement of shipping and the harbor, the spatial expanse of the broad river, and the artful molding of the landscape and what humans have done with it into a connective tissue, the Erasmus Bridge has few peers among recent bridge designs.

Top left:
Detail of abutment and cable anchoring

Bottom left:
Pedestrian approach and abutment

Top right:
Diagram of drawbridge portion

Bottom right:
Continuation of public space under bridge abutment

1992–1994 ▸ Villa Wilbrink
Amersfoort, The Netherlands

Opposite page:
View from rear garden

Villa Wilbrink grows out of the ground. Faced with a new neighborhood on what had been an empty meadow in a suburb of Amersfoort, both client and architect felt the need to close themselves off from whatever might develop around them while recalling the site's expansive horizontality. The solution is a house that rises slowly out of the street and front yard as a gravel-covered sloped plane. A slot in the middle of this diagonal roof lets one drive up to the garage door and enter into the house. The house thus turns its back on the neighbors by hiding part of the area's infrastructure of roads and driveways, while providing the inhabitants with a maintenance-free front yard.

Entrance area and carport

Once inside, Villa Wilbrink opens up. The modest villa's 1,615 sq. ft. of living space groups around a patio between the garage and the house's main bulk. The shared bathrooms protrude from the long façade as a curved wooden volume that closes the patio off from the neighbors to the South.

On the inside, the house consists of one living area and a row of three small bedrooms along a dead-end corridor. A large window looks out towards the gravel-covered backyard, which is empty except for a small grove of trees. Bedroom windows

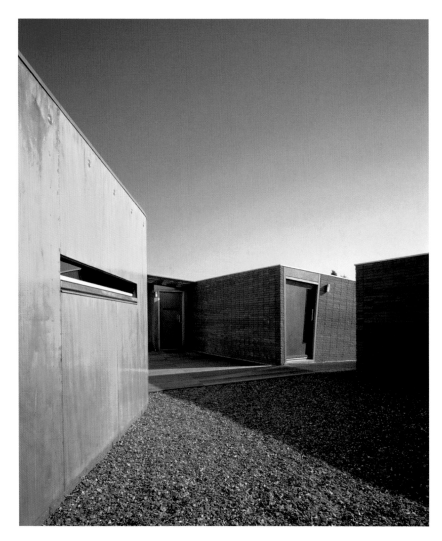

Left:
Courtyard with bathroom to left

Bottom left:
Plan

Bottom right:
Living room

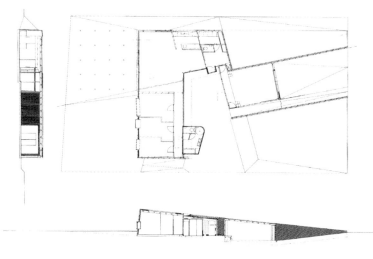

Courtyard from sloped front garden

framed in wood give pattern and scale to the rear façade. To emphasize the sense of excavation, the architects faced this one vertical plane with limestone blocks glued onto the concrete frame. At the corner, the architects further emphasized the sense that the living areas are like a cave under a plane lifted out of the ground by inserting a corner window from the ground to a height of almost 5 ft., so that one can only look out by sitting or lying down.

1993–1998 ▸ Möbius House
Het Gooi, The Netherlands

Opposite page:
The stairs in the center of the house

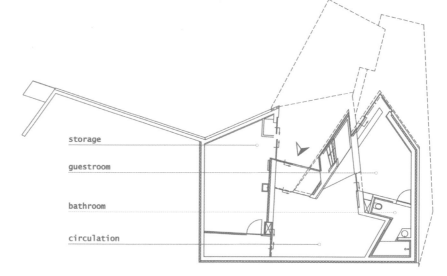

storage

guestroom

bathroom

circulation

Right:
Plan of lower level

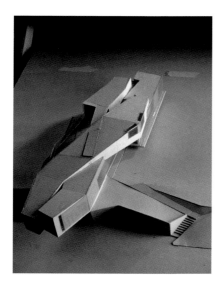

Model showing the interlocking volumes of
the various living areas

The Möbius House is van Berkel and Bos' most ambitious residential project to date, both in scale and as an expression of a theoretical position. Located in one of the most exclusive neighborhoods in the Netherlands, it is a freestanding concrete object that acts as a residential knot in an expansive site sweeping from the side of a modest rise down to a nearby lake.

As a model for this knot van Berkel and Bos used a geometric shape that had long fascinated them, the so-called Möbius strip. This double-looped torus forms a continuous plane as it sweeps through its figure-eight form. The architects connected what was to them an emblem of the kind of continuous and autonomous space they wished to unfold out of the world around them with the clients' desire for a house that would respond to the 24-hour rhythms of their lives.

Inhabited by a working couple and occasionally by their grown children, the Möbius House consists of a more or less standard program the architects strung out in both a horizontal and vertical direction. After one drives through the property and sweeps by the building's façade of concrete volumes seeming to balance on glass, one enters in the middle at the structure's rear, interrupting the flow at its midpoint. One bedroom and one studio are to the right at a lower level; another pair is up and to the left. More stairs and ramps than are strictly necessary connect these far-flung points of repose around shared living areas.

The idea is that the inhabitants cross and re-cross the house in both a horizontal and vertical axis during the course of the day, meeting up to share meals or conversation, while encountering outside guests at the midpoints of their diurnal journeys. Two smaller bedrooms together with a kitchen area support this fluid spine of spaces.

View from north into kitchen area

Bottom:
Exploded section, showing use pattern

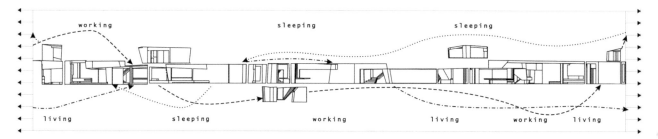

View from south

Van Berkel and Bos conceived the whole house as concrete monolith that, in the course of becoming distended and involuted, has broken apart into a series of splayed, angled and cantilevered volumes. Wood covers the ceiling in the main living area and forms balustrades, but in the remainder of the house, the living volumes are carved out of the space between concrete planes and extend out through glass walls.

Conceived as a single and continuous shape, the Möbius House is in fact a collection of fragments that rearranges a residential program as a collage. More than the organizational innovation of the house's floor plan, it is the intricacies of composition in this plastic whole that give the structure its power. It is the non-stop realization of architecture as the play of pure forms in light, not the rollercoaster of a 24/7 life, that surrounds one in the Möbius House.

View from living room towards upper level

Left:
Plan of main level

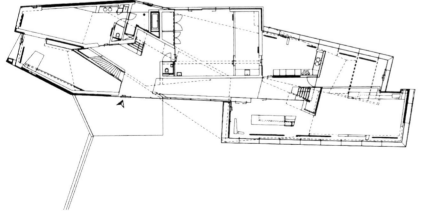

View of stairs

Left:
Plan of upper level

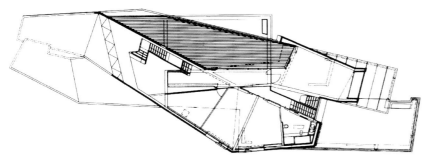

1995–1998 ▸ Bascule Bridge & Bridge Master's House

Purmerend, The Netherlands

Opposite page:
View of Bridge Master's House

Right:
Night view

Bottom:
Plan

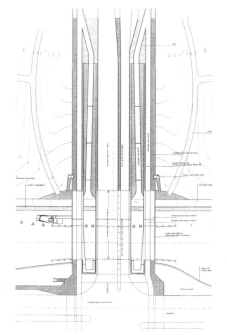

Infrastructure is not something we usually think much about or even see. It is either underground or part of the systems of transportation we use in our little well-designed bubbles. Van Berkel and Bos, however, have made the manipulation of transportation nodes one of their specialties, and this is one of their finer designs.

The bridge connects the old downtown of this city about half an hour north of Amsterdam with the large new bedroom communities that have grown up around it. As with the Erasmus Bridge, each form of transportation (car, bicycle, pedestrian) has its own expression, but here in the form of separate, parallel bridges that can be raised to allow boats to pass.

Controlling this choreography of infrastructure is the Bridge Master. He resides in a skewed, canted construction 33 ft. high. Its concrete structure is clad completely with expanded metal mesh. As a result, one can see through the structure at times, while at other times the object becomes massive and impenetrable. While the object is eminently practical, providing the Master with a view while remaining shaded and protecting the service areas with a fence-like structure, the building's main contribution to its surroundings is to turn mute infrastructure into an expressive monument.

1995–1999 ▸ Het Valkhof Museum
Nijmegen, The Netherlands

Opposite page:
View of front façade from northeast

The Netherlands is an extremely flat area. It is that horizontal distention that makes the site where the Romans founded what is today the city of Nijmegen all the more remarkable. Valkhof Hill rises next to the Rhine River and dominates the surrounding landscape. On the slope of this hill van Berkel and Bos designed the Het Valkhof Museum as a place to become aware of both the history and the geography of the site. The museum is a machine for understanding where one is.

The site is also adjacent to Nijmegen's main market square, which sits on top of a parking garage. Van Berkel and Bos answered this horizontal plane with a simple vertical façade of glass placed against blue panels. This strip, which comes apart into slightly splayed lines, hovers over a transparent glass base and just under the line of the trees on the hill beyond it, as if it were a measuring the place's height. It creates a sense of calm and focus on the square's northern edge, acting as an abstraction of the sort of monumental façade one would expect from a museum.

One enters by first passing under and then ascending a broad flight of stairs that continues on the building's interior, becomes covered in wood, splits and then extends all the way to the site's rear where one faces the back of the hill. These stairs are the Museum's central organizing space as well as its structural core, anchoring the light volumes that extend to either side of the central structure.

Front façade from market square

39

Entrance stairs, looking towards rear

One then turns and enters the gallery sequence. It is a single floor of almost 21,530 sq. ft. with galleries that are nearly 10 ft. high. Here one is guided through the collections of everything from Roman to contemporary art by the wavy ceiling, behind which one can just glimpse the technical systems and structure that allow these open spaces to exist and be inhabited. Meanwhile one can also look out from all the rear galleries at the hill. One can wander through the past and understand its relation to site, and one can give oneself over to the new realm opened up by the abstract and rational architecture.

Galleries with "wave" ceiling and glass walls

Bottom left:
Rear façade

Bottom right:
Section through stair hall, looking north

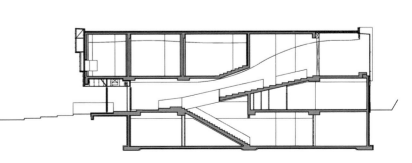

1995–2000 ▸ Chapel
Hilversum, The Netherlands

Opposite page:
Main hall with colored walls of skylight

Right:
Model of major walls and skylights

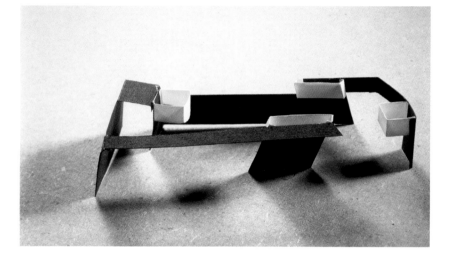

Rear view, showing Profilit glass panels and office windows above

On the outside, this appears to be just a simple box. Only the relentless minimalism of the façade, made up of Profilit glass channels punctured now and then by regular windows, gives the sense that this is a place of some importance. Set back from the street, its siting, materiality, and abstraction remove it from the everyday life of the small provincial city of Hilversum.

It is only after one enters through a slightly indented part of the façade, walks down a corridor and then turns that one realizes where one is: a place of worship, serene, tall and white, washed by light from both skylights and the glass-paneled walls. The room, 82 by 50 ft. in plan, is close to 20 ft. tall, and the skylights rise another 13 ft. beyond this. The side walls of these skylights are painted a deep red, balancing the greenish glow from the glass panels.

Beyond this space there is not much to this chapel serving two Protestant denominations that merged. The offices and other ancillary functions are hidden on the second floor, while public services are on the other side of the corridor. A slight skew of the façade serves to further remove the interior space from the outside and sets off the use from the building's structure. Here is a place for contemplation freed completely by and through architecture.

1997–2000 ▸ NMR Facility

Utrecht University, Utrecht, The Netherlands

Opposite page:
View from northeast

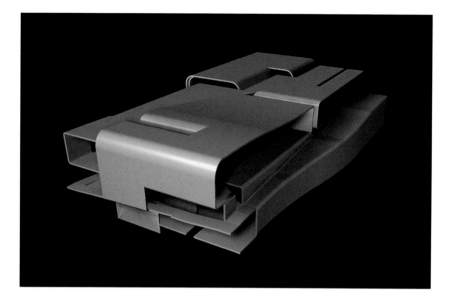

Right:
Model of continuous surfaces

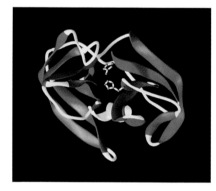

Diagram of continuous surfaces

This is a highly technical building that also continues a development in architecture that one might think of as purely formal. The Neutron Magnetic Resonance (NMR) Facility at the University of Utrecht houses eight spectrometers whose powerful magnetic forces cannot be disturbed without hindering the experiments. This means that even the electrical current generated by elevators is undesirable. Moreover, the work these magnets do is by its nature invisible and mysterious, as it takes place at a molecular level.

What then should be the character of a building that has no function that can be seen? Van Berkel and Bos' answer was to design a composition that makes us aware of what is being hidden and what is visible.

The NMR Facility is essentially a 353,150-cu.-ft. structure formed by a series of concrete shells that contain the machinery and their ancillary equipment. Ramps rather than elevators connect the machine rooms on two levels. Glass panels set flush to the surface without visible moldings and covered with a fret pattern light the circulation areas, such as the ramps, as well as the offices and smaller laboratories that make up half the square footage.

Thus the building presents itself as a series of interlocking concrete and glass planes. The concrete, however, is continuous from floor to wall to ceiling, making the NMR Facility a so-called "single surface" building. One of the first such structures to be realized, the Educatorium designed by Rem Koolhaas, sits adjacent to this modest structure, and van Berkel and Bos consciously sought to continue this experiment in breaking through the traditional dichotomy between horizontal and vertical surfaces. In this case, as the architects had pointed out, the surfaces are also completely

Front façade

structural. For this reason, no ancillary structure is needed. There are furthermore no columns to interrupt the laboratories' smooth flow.

Van Berkel and Bos placed the building's largest space, a double-height laboratory, to the rear of the building, anchoring the structure in a sea of monotonous high-rise buildings while allowing for easy servicing. The laboratory's front presents a balanced mix of concrete and glass elements, giving one a sense of the relationship between enclosed and open spaces. Along the side, the ramp connecting the two floors bows out slightly and is visible from the outside. There the scientists can look out and simultaneously be on view, as van Berkel and Bos illustrated by documenting the building with mannequins posed in these spaces. Thus the message of the NMR Facility seems to be that architecture allows one to play hide-and-seek with science. The building occludes and protects both us and its equipment, and reveals tantalizing fragments of the work that otherwise is invisible by its very nature.

Side view, showing major laboratory

Right:
Plan

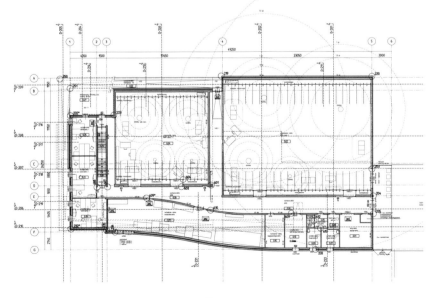

1997–2002 ▸ Electrical Substation
Innsbruck, Austria

Opposite page:
View from courtyard

Right:
View from southwest

Interior view

Like a domesticated beast, the Electrical Substation occupies a leftover lot in Innsbruck's historic core. Instead of trying to hide this bit of infrastructure, van Berkel and Bos decided to give it a clear and complex presence. Clad in basalt lava, it is a complex construction that twists and turns around its mysterious functions in such a manner as to break down the scale of what would otherwise be an alien being.

The architects see the Substation as "hump in the landscape." They devised a molded concrete plinth that also allows for future expansion. It rises up, folds and indents to allow programmatic spaces that are actually occupied by human beings to nestle in and under the enclosure for technical equipment. The wrapping functions also serve to give the building a further sense of scale, as strips and planes of windows break up the stone volume and allow light to penetrate into the mass.

While the technical requirements for such buildings are demanding, van Berkel and Bos both here and in their first such structure, in Amersfoort, used what freedom they had to manipulate the building's surface and mass and turn them into sculpture: active participants in the urban scene that come between our bodies and the larger, function-driven objects that make up the city.

1998–2003 ▸ Prince Claus Bridge
Utrecht, The Netherlands

Opposite page:
View from east

Right:
View of "knot" under bridge

Wire model of pylon

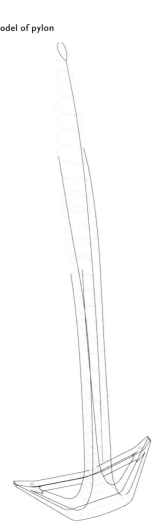

Rising from a steel "knot" that anchors and supports the whole structure, the single pylon supporting the Prince Claus Bridge turns from a rectangular structure into a an oval one, narrowing and then thickening to sprout a fanned array of cable stays before tapering off to a point. This single form combines within it many of the shapes in the earlier design of the Erasmus Bridge, here condensed into a singular statement for a much smaller bridge.

One of the main reasons for the reliance on one, albeit complex, form was the fact that this was a "design/build" project, so that van Berkel and Bos had no control over how the bridge would be detailed and built. They chose to make something as simple as possible: a single roadway, split (as in the Rotterdam Bridge) by the pylon, from which the horizontal surface hangs. The whole construction is stabilized by the splayed form of the steel truss below, which also serves to open up space for the public path that passes underneath the bridge. Painted a pale purplish blue, the bridge is little more than one carefully controlled gesture that evades definition as it changes shape and color as one moves around it, while enabling one to understand its simple structural logic.

1999–2001 ▸ Water Villas
Almere, The Netherlands

The Dutch have produced some of the best mass-produced and social housing in the world. However, many of the inhabitants of these modern machines for living complain of the monotony and facelessness of boxes strung out in suburban meadows. Produced mainly as poured-in-place concrete "tunnels" of a standard dimension (11.5 by 16.4 ft.), these row-house elements only entertain slight variations in cladding and arrangements.

In the new town of Almere, a bedroom community of almost 200,000 inhabitants on what was, until forty years ago, a seabed, the municipality wanted to see if it could create a sense of variety by asking architects to come up with other ways of both arranging the "tunnels" and giving inhabitants a chance to customize their homes. Several architects were given the opportunity to create examples of such semi-standardized versions of what the Dutch call "wild living."

The response of van Berkel and Bos to this challenge was to create 48 "water villas" whose variety comes from stacking the basic elements on top of each other in a shifting pattern. In addition, the inhabitants also have the opportunity to add a steel "cage" that can be variously used as a room extension or even as a balcony. While the basic home has a floor area of 1,615 sq. ft., the extensions can increase that total to 1,775 or even 1,940 sq. ft.

View of singular unit with glassed-in porch additions

The basic house consists of three floors of bare, tunnel-like space completely formed by concrete. Twenty of the villas form rows, the remainder are free-standing. The buildings' exteriors are finished in anthracite tiles that give the homes a sense of solidity, while the extensions are covered with copper-colored metallic plates. Inhabitants are free to arrange the spaces as they see fit, though in reality the ground floor is usually one open living area, while the second floor is divided up to create two or three bedrooms and the top level becomes either a master bedroom or an extra work area. All of the metal boxes have been enclosed and are used as room extensions.

By shifting the various floors in relation to each other, van Berkel and Bos give the impression that the whole neighborhood is a free arrangement of boxes. This sense of freedom and play belies the standard materials and dimensions of each individual element. The compositions are, in fact, carefully considered so as to maximize both privacy and views as much as possible. Pushing and pulling at standardized building practices while using the efficiency created by a construction industry that produces affordable housing for (almost) all Dutch people, van Berkel and Bos have created a neighborhood that gives one the sense that the facts of life could be arranged in a different manner.

Overall view

Opposite page top:
View of row houses

Opposite page bottom:
Plan

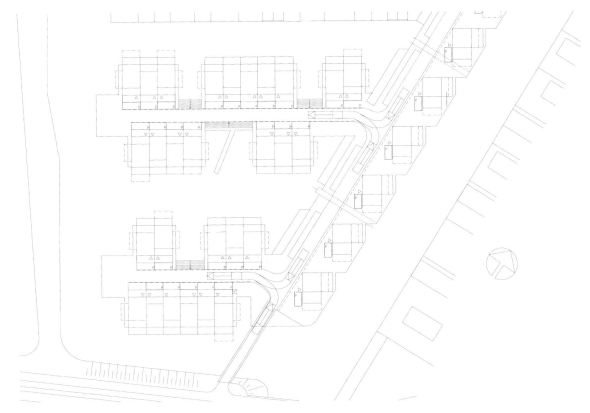

1999–2004 ▸ La Defense Offices
Almere, The Netherlands

Opposite page:
View of courtyard

Right:
Model view in context

Reflective and prismatic interior façade

The La Defense Office building is at first glance a suburban office park like any other. Sitting on top of a pancake of structured parking, the development's three to six-storey blocks turn their back on the surroundings, presenting a slick façade of aluminum and silver-tinted glass panels to their neighbors. True, this is a building that is sleeker than most, with much care spent on binding the various elements of the façade together into a taut skin that lets one understand where the floors are (through bands of ribbon windows), while shaping the whole into a mass. True, the building does open up at both the corner facing the nearby downtown and on the other side to a public park, with broad steps that invite one to enter.

But the real sense of difference comes from the flashes of color that one sees only in passing from the outside. These indicate first of all that this is not an ordinary block of offices. Van Berkel and Bos treated the whole nearly 250,000-sq.-ft. development as a block and then pulled it apart to fill out the site completely, leaving what appear to be tear marks in the middle. This act of separation turns the offices into thin fingers, so that light can enter the offices from all sides. It also creates sheltered courtyards where workers can gather. The building masses up towards its center, giving La Defense a sense of being more like an artificial piece of landscape—a small hill—than the orthogonal blocks that surround its sloped and angled façades.

The building's greatest innovation comes from the material the architects chose to cover the interior façades of the office building complex. It is a film, developed by the

Courtyard view

American firm 3M, that until now was used mainly for packaging. Highly reflective and prismatic, it seems to change color both as one walks by and as the sun moves across the sky. Thus one gains a sense of place as one moves through La Defense, and a sense of time as one works there. The molten lava at the heart of this human-made, fractured mountain tells us where we are in a world of artifice.

View of passage under "tooth" between
courtyards

Plan in urban context

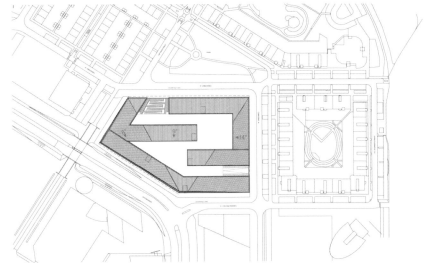

2000-2003 ▸ Living Tomorrow Pavilion
Amsterdam, The Netherlands

Opposite page:
Interior view

Right:
Side view

Landing Gallery/Foyer Loges
Garden
Offices/Boardroom
Service/Utilities
House of the Future
Business Department of the Future
Office of the Future Prototype
Auditorium
Reception lobby
Event-space

Diagram of functions and circulation

What kind of space will we inhabit tomorrow? Van Berkel and Bos believe it is a Klein bottle. This fluid container that wraps itself inside-out became their model when they were asked to create a semi-permanent pavilion that would be used to showcase sponsored exhibitions of the new equipment and technology manufacturers wish to present as representing the future.

The Living Tomorrow Pavilion is situated in an anonymous district of office buildings outside of Amsterdam. The object is covered in blue-painted corrugated metal patterns. Though it is only 148 ft. high, its fluid shapes, consisting of a vertical exhibition area, which faces the street and a lower element housing auditorium and introductory spaces to the rear, stand out starkly from the anonymous structures around this pavilion.

Inside, the equally curvaceous forms flow into each other. They are segmented into painted bands rather than into anything as conventional as walls, floors and ceilings. Perhaps more science fiction than prognosis, the Living Tomorrow Pavilion promises a stylish departure from current conditions.

2000–2003 › Hotel Castell
Zuoz, Switzerland

Opposite page:
South façade of new apartment bloc

Right:
View of typical solarium

Plan

The cave and the promontory combine in this hybrid program for apartments and a "hammam," or Arabic bath, high in the Swiss Alps. The addition also includes the renovation of the existing Hotel Castell, a luxury resort the owner has turned into the site for his art collection and site-specific installations.

The renovated rooms are spaces of sparse white planes with a few wood accents that give prominence to the views out the windows. Van Berkel and Bos perceive the new apartment building, which sits a few yards apart from the brick-covered hotel, as modern interlocking spaces that trace the existing topography. The simple, rectangular building curves slightly to follow the hillside. Bedrooms shelter to the rear, on the north side, while living spaces open up to the view and the southern sun. The apartments closest to the existing hotel have glass-fronted solaria, while the units on the west half open up to balconies. The slabs supporting these open extensions slot into the space between the solaria next to them, thus enforcing the sense of a single volume undergoing a transformation as it moves across the site. Beyond this manipulation of the volume, the apartments are a simple glass volume with a poured-in-place concrete structure hovering over a base enclosed with metal mesh.

While the apartment building looks outward, the hammam is hidden in the hillside. The architects responded to the tradition of domes and tiled volumes by dividing the space with five luminous columns, lit in shades of purple, blue and mauve. These spatial dividers also hide the structural columns. The floors and walls are covered in tile. They curve continuously and sensually, transforming the hotel's basement into a cave that echoes the naked human body.

2000-2006 ▸ VilLA NM

Upstate New York, USA

Opposite page:
View from south

Right:
West view, showing carport with bedroom above

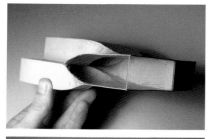

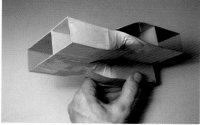

Conceptual models

For many years during the 1990s, van Berkel and Bos claimed that they were "navigating between the blob and the box." By this they meant that they were interested both in pulling apart, deforming and reassembling standard building components, and in the manner in which computer-generated forms could create fluid shapes. In this house, they have finally combined the two by assigning the box to the living areas and connecting them with a continuous surface that serves as this modest structure's main circulation area.

Sited on a ridge in upstate New York, this nearly 2,700-sq.-ft. vacation retreat is essentially a twist on the split-level home developed in California in the 1950s as a way of differentiating in a non-hierarchical manner between public and private spaces in the house. Here, the parking and kitchen area are at the lowest level. One enters, as in any suburban home, through the kitchen, and then goes up a staircase around which the floors of that first area twist and turn into supports for the circulation and then into the ceilings for the intermediate and second floors. Along the way, one has a view of the surrounding countryside one is moving to surmount. The living room encompasses a large volume with floor-to-ceiling windows on two sides, and a small guest bedroom off to the east side. One re-enters the "twist" to rise up to the bedroom suite on the highest level, which hovers over the parking area on v-shaped columns.

The house is an efficient warping of residential traditions. While it appears from its short façades as a modest modernist box, from the long sides the concrete deformation becomes visible. It appears as an abstraction of the site's geography. This is

View from living room to kitchen and upper
level

Right:
Bathroom under "twist"

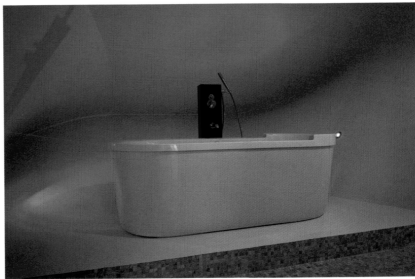

also the infrastructural part of the house, where circulation, kitchen and bathrooms come together, as in the center of a traditional house. It is as if van Berkel and Bos had taken Frank Lloyd Wright's famous call to "break the box" of the suburban home by extruding living spaces out from a central core into the landscape and replaced it with the notion that one can "warp the box" to achieve the same end.

View of entrance along "twist" to living room

2001–2006 ▸ Mercedes-Benz Museum
Stuttgart, Germany

Opposite page:
Detail view of façade

Right:
Model of typical gallery with sweeping ramp

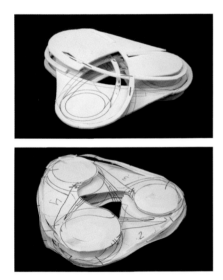

Conceptual models

The Mercedes-Benz Museum in Stuttgart is without a doubt van Berkel and Bos' most complete and important building to date. As an icon of mobility, technology and status, a complex machine for circulation integrated with structure, and a continuous unfolding of spaces that break through the usual hierarchies one expects in an autonomous building, the museum makes clear how this firm is trying to make a case for architecture as a spatial and material criticism of our current culture.

The Mercedes-Benz Museum sits on Stuttgart's outskirts, where it must compete for attention with the adjacent car factory, an elevated highway, a soccer stadium and nearby gas storage tanks. Van Berkel and Bos' response, though internally generated, is a hybrid between all of these fluid and inward-turned shapes, as well as an abstraction of the hills rising next to the site. The building's shape is in fact a double helix pulled slightly apart. The ramps in this system cross and re-cross each other around a central void, while forming two secondary void spaces for larger exhibitions. The resulting three-lobed form resembles a stretched and warped cylinder. The architects made the motion of the ramps visible as slots of windows between the metal cladding of the galleries, so that the whole building appears to be stretching apart with the energy of the movement inside. Sited on a plinth and without a clearly expressed base or crown, the Mercedes-Benz Museum is a solid form deformed to the point that it has no particular references to, but can hold its own within, this confusing landscape.

It is perhaps not an accident that the floor plan resembles the three-pronged star that is the car company's symbol. Van Berkel and Bos claim this is accidental (or intuitive), as the form was generated from the Möbius strip they used before, here stretched out both vertically and horizontally and doubled to allow for two different circulation paths. One of these is a straight historic progression of automobiles ("collections"), the other a focus on the themes and associations the car has called up over the years ("myths"). One starts one's experience by entering the 6-storey lobby, where one looks up at the three-pronged star that serves as the main distribution

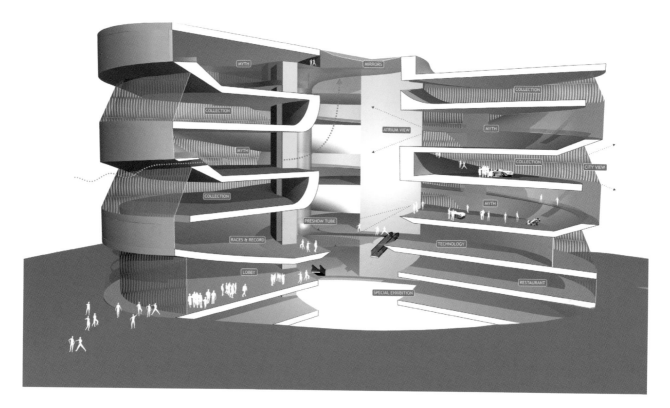

element for people and structure at the building's top. Overscaled and futuristically styled elevators take one to that top level, from which one can choose which of the two paths one wants to follow.

The museum's structural gymnastics, developed in collaboration with local engineer Werner Sobek, reveal themselves as one progresses through its spaces. As one slowly descends down either path, the concrete ramp on which one is walking rises up above one, twisting and turning to become the ceiling overhead. Instead of moving from floor to floor or room to room, one experiences a continual unfolding of space. Angled columns along the windows reinforce the sense that space has opened up in structure through movement, rather than the building enclosing static space. Van Berkel and Bos curved every surface they could, even stretching the plaster ceiling to allow for indentations where technical systems and lights need to penetrate this fluid form.

The exhibition designs, created by collaborator Hans-Günther Mertz, manage to stage the history and themes Mercedes-Benz wishes visitors to learn about in a manner that makes full use of the pulsating width and height or spaces the architecture opens up. The collection and myth areas each occupy different lobes, and Mertz

Section perspective, showing exhibition areas and circulation

Detail section of façade

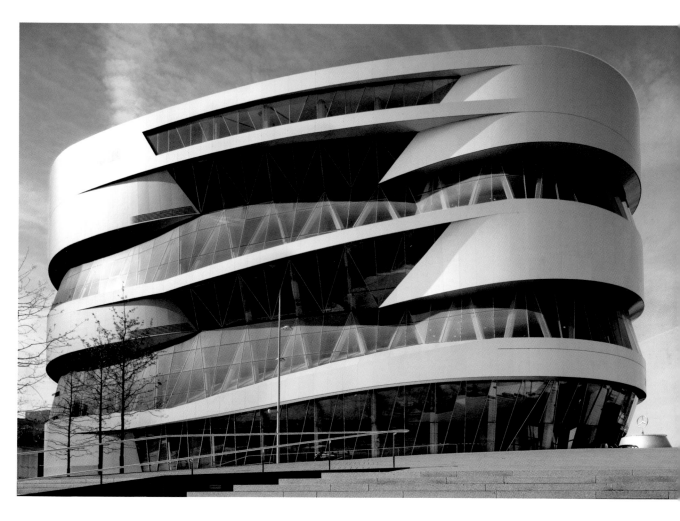

View from entrance plaza

Left:
Plan level 1

Opposite page:
View of central atrium with elevators and "twist"

Right:
View of first historical gallery

Bottom:
Escalator from level 1 leading to shopping area and "passage"

has used the larger spaces one keeps reentering to create dramatic stage sets. These become more and more intense as one descends, culminating in a space where the ramps reintegrate and merge into ramps ascending onto the walls, where racing cars zoom off into space. One then leaves the continual system and descends a bright orange staircase through the theater of speed to enter the shop area. This space, designed by the Dutch firm Concrete, dissolves the museum's curved forms into translucent curtains screening the merchandise. Perhaps the project's largest disappointment is that one exits through a car showroom that van Berkel and Bos did not design. This space seems to belie the project's supra-commercial pretentions.

At once heroic and theatrical, the Mercedes-Benz Museum brings the notion of the monumental back into architecture. As that which fixes in time and place the memories and values of those who commission such structures, the monumental has the quality of the iconic, the autonomous and that which is larger than life, while at the same time it fixes the site and reminds one of the traditions out of which it came and which it seeks to embody. This is a thoroughly modern monument, however. It is an abstract, enigmatic and taut container for continuous space that just happens to exhibit the history of a particular kind of automobile.

2002–2004 ▸ Galleria Department Store
Seoul, South Korea

Opposite page:
View of central atrium

nt:

...ical store floor, with **circulation** lines and directional lighting

The shimmering mutability of fashion's surfaces are the theme in this extensive remodeling of one of the major department stores in Seoul, South Korea. The exterior has been turned into an abstract cloak of glass disks that change color continually, while the interior has dissolved into a collection of catwalks on which one becomes the subject of appraisal along with the clothes one can buy in the store.

The Galleria had a reputation for being innovative and trendsetting, but the owners also wanted to give it a certain elegance that would anchor the continually changing images their simple block housed. Van Berkel and Bos responded first by stripping the façade and attaching 4,330 glass disks to the metal substructure. Each of these disks, which overlap each other in the manner of the fish scales they resemble, is coated with an iridescent film, so that they change color as one moves by them or the light changes (a technique the architects developed in the La Defense office building). At night, the colors are meant to reflect the previous day's weather conditions, which have been stored on a computer. Designed in collaboration with Arup Lighting, this system turns what was a simple container into a statement about the mutability and the attractiveness of pure clothing. One overscaled window in the store's main façade conveys the notion that this is a place that one can buy something, not just a building turned into a mannequin.

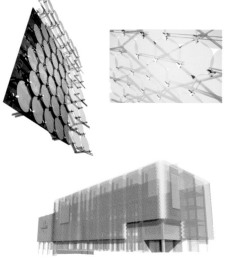

Details of façade construction, showing glass disks

In keeping with this approach, the architects left the bulk of the interior as it was, dominated by stand-alone boutiques presenting a changing array of products. Instead of trying to reinvent shopping, they concentrated on the circulation elements that lead one through the store. The major atrium space became a kaleidoscopic experience because they clad the escalators, the walls and the ceilings with glass that is either reflective or opaque. This dissolves the solid forms in the space, reflects the shopper among the various goods, and emphasizes views out onto the selling areas.

One moves through these floors along what van Berkel and Bos call "catwalks": curving walkways with shiny white floors and ceilings. Recessed fluorescent tubes provide continuous lighting paths that are also gently tinted by the application of color to the coves. Stripes on the floor echo these bands of light above. As much as possible, the architects hid all structure and furniture behind reflective and curving surfaces.

The notion of "streamlining" was launched by the designer Raymond Loewy to "remove all barriers between the product and the shopper." Here van Berkel and Bos have taken that industrial design idea to the level of architecture, dissolving the building into skin and surface and setting both desirer and what is desired afloat while providing clear lanes along which one should stream through this consumer world.

2002–2007 ▸ Agora Theater
Lelystad, The Netherlands

Exterior view

Opposite page top:
View of main theater

Opposite page bottom:
Massing models

By placing a large theater seating 750 people at a right angle to a smaller, flexible theater for 200 people hovering over the entrance, van Berkel and Bos have created a sense of drama that extends from the stage out into the urban area in which this provincial performing arts center is placed.

Both projects' two major elements are more or less conventional, though the architects took pains to make the main theater as intimate as possible through wide aisles and a horseshoe balcony hovering close to the stage. One enters the Agora from the main public square in this new town, which was not founded until just before the Second World War. The secondary theater space presents itself as a billboard and shelters the glass-fronted public entrance. The main theater is straight ahead, and the public space develops into a multi-functional area (which can be segmented off for meetings) wrapping the Agora's west façade.

In combining these various elements into a single building, van Berkel and Bos have stretched and folded the Agora's metal skin so that it seems to be bulging out on all sides. The main stair tower and the loading dock escape from the main volume, pinning the whole complex down to the ground. A continual handrail that runs from the outside along the stairs and up to the roof emphasizes the architects' desire to let the exploration of these spaces be the main theatrical event one experiences in and through the volumes they have enclosed.

2004–2006 ▸ Tea House on Bunker
Vreeland, The Netherlands

View of rear from approach
The new building sits partly on top of the existing bunker.

Like a giant, geometric Cyclops' eye, this Tea House turns towards a polo field that occupies one corner of a wealthy businessman's estate. Intended as a place to view the games, it is also a folly in the tradition of such garden structures meant to express aristocrats' fantasies about their place in the world.

The building's foundations consist of a bunker built in 1936. It was part of an extensive defensive system the Dutch built to ward off attack from the east (Germany), but that proved wholly ineffective. The remaining fragments are now monuments and thus had to be preserved. The Tea House twists and cantilevers away from this modest, concrete base in a single steel-framed and metal-clad splayed form that looks out toward what were once grazing grounds and are now the playing fields.

From the rear, one can still recognize the bunker's original shape, with its sloped roof and rectangular base. Van Berkel and Bos then folded and angled these shapes,

View from polo grounds to viewing space

flipping them, drawing them out and enlarging their scale to effect an enclosure for a new use that looks out rather than hunkers down. The process is one that they developed in their extrusion of forms through computer modeling, but here it is carried out in sharp geometries that are more aggressive and exuberant.

As a folly, the Tea House has no function other than to allow the users to gather in its upstairs space, on a wood floor and under the metal trusses, to look out through the floor-to-ceiling glass. Additional structures may join the Tea House as the owner develops his estate into a business retreat center, but for now this object stands as a monument to the spectacular and the spectacle rising up out of the productive earth and the defensive past.

Current projects

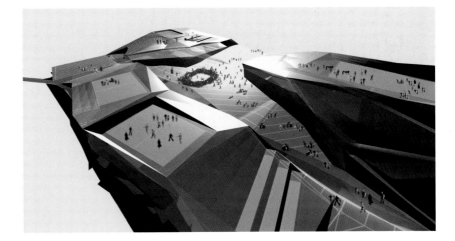

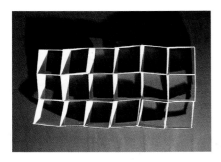

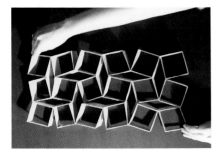

Ponte Parodi, Genoa, Italy, 2001–2009
Conceptual models

Over the last few decades, UNStudio has developed into an international organization. Not only do the designers have commissions all over the world, from the United States to Asia to the Gulf Region, but their team consists of a group of collaborators from around the globe. English is the language spoken in this office and among the consultants who also reside all over the globe.

The scale of UNStudio's projects is also growing. The most ambitious of all the ones currently on the boards (or in the computers) is the Ponte Parodi, a mixed-use development that has been in the works since 2002. It is meant to replace a pier in the port of Genoa with a combination of entertainment, sports, shopping and wellness facilities. The architects won the competition with the design for a "piazza on the Mediterranean" that would draw the activities of the city out into the water. Diamond-shaped cuts through the program areas will create smaller gathering spaces and bring light into the large building blocks. When constructed, Ponte Parodi will clearly show the firm's approach to urbanism as a drawing together, intensification and monumentalization of the city's activities. In fact, the difference between urban nodes and buildings becomes indistinct in their approach, as presaged by the design for the Arnhem Train Station Development, which will be completed by 2010. Infrastructure, whether it is a multi-nodal transit station or a quay, provides a knot bringing people together and into contact with the most physical part of their human-made environment. Forms develop from these knots and shelter spaces of communal use.

This approach is also clear in such large-scale structures as the Wien Mitte complex, where an existing station has been excavated and used as the basis for an immense, funnel-shaped void. Building masses tend towards the site's corner, where they help to connect with and reinforce the urban blocks around the station. Thus infrastructure explodes outward, creating an interior version of the public void at the traditional city's core, and then subsides into a new scale and intensity of development.

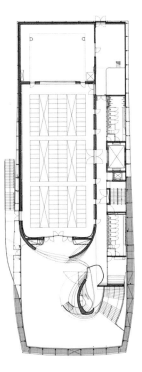

Top:
Music Theater, Graz, Austria, 1998–2007
Plan

In the Battersea Weave office complex, infrastructure is respected, folded and reiterated as new buildings. Set on the southwest corner of a massive redevelopment of the old power station on London's South Bank, this glass-enclosed string of office floors follows the adjacent elevated train line and then turns away around vertical circulation cores to unfold almost 550,000 sq. ft. of flexible rentable space. Angled and continually in motion, the building seeks to open up the dark, closed forms of the site into something extended and extensive, enclosed with structure that is stretched taut.

That sense of opening space that seeks to extend beyond the confines of structure from an infrastructural base is evident in almost all of UNStudio's recent large-scale projects. It is even evident in some of their smaller residential work. Along with this exuberant pushing at the box, however, the firm has also continued to develop its interest in the deformation and involution of solid forms. The trifoil plan of the Mercedes Benz Museum shows up again as an apartment building in Busan, South Korea, and the continuous surface loops through even such modest projects as the renovation of the Jewish Museum in Amsterdam.

In the Music Theater in Graz, a project already twice postponed but now underway, UNStudio ponders once again how the blob and the box can come together. Here the answer is that the two can be melded by twisting the interior container for the theater into contact with its fluid wrapper through a vertical circulation element that also acts as a major structural core. The solid object of the theater transforms into a transparent container that invites the city into the building's heart.

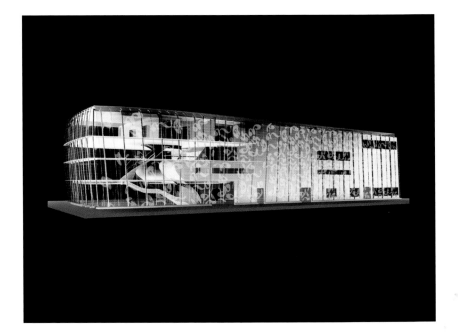

Music Theater, Graz, Austria, 1998–2007
Model view

Battersea Weave Office Building, London, Great Britain, 2004–2010
View from plaza

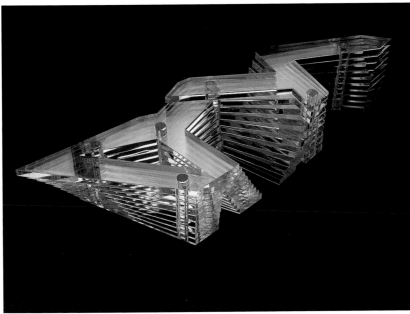

Battersea Weave Office Building, London, Great Britain, 2004–2010
Diagram model

Te Papa Museum, Wellington, New Zealand, 2006–2010
View from park

Right:
Te Papa Museum, Wellington, New Zealand, 2006–2010
Plans of entrance and typical gallery level

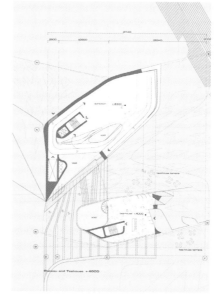

Residential Tower, Busan, Seoul, South Korea, 2006–2009
View of complete project

UNStudio's most interesting current project is the extension of the Te Papa Museum in Wellington, New Zealand. The building combines elements of the continual spirals of the Mercedes Benz Museum with the unfolding out of space from a central structural and circulation core that they have used in projects that they sought to anchor in urban and physical realities. Projecting out towards the adjacent park from a solid street wall with two splayed arms, the museum extension invites its public into a series of shifting plazas that move up through the building and allow the objects on display to be seen from many different angles.

Working at a variety of scales for different programs all over the world, UNStudio finds anchors in their work in the continual pushing of programmatic demands and structural possibilities to create spaces that are as open, fluid, and dramatic as possible. Instead of letting these structures dissolve or explode into almost nothing, they work hard to shape buildings that have a sense of solidity that serves to mark place, contain space and pose the presence of the institutions they house.

Partners and Projects

The partners and staff of UNStudio during the design process, showing their collaborative working method. Ben van Berkel, (Co-founder/Principal Architect), Caroline Bos (Co-founder/Director), Harm Wassink (Partner/Senior Architect), Gerard Loozekoot (Associate Director/Senior Architect), Astrid Piber (Associate Director/Senior Architect)

1989–1993 Electrical Substation, Amersfoort, The Netherlands
Client: Regionale Energie Maatschappij Utrecht (REMU)
Program: 50/10 kV substation
Gross floor surface: 16,361 sq.ft.
Volume: 5,886 cu.yd.
Design UNStudio: Ben van Berkel with Harrie Pappot and Pieter Koster, Hugo Beschoor Plug, Jaap Punt, Rik van Dolderen
Engineering: Hollandsche Beton Maatschappij, Rijswijk

1990–1992 Karbouw Offices, Amersfoort, The Netherlands
Client: Schipper Bosch Projectontwikkeling, Amersfoort
Gross floor surface: 12,432 sq.ft.
Design UNStudio: Ben van Berkel with Aad Krom Kasper Aussems, Frank Verhoeven, Stephan de Bever
Engineering: Buro Bouwpartners, Hilversum

1990–1996 Erasmus Bridge, Rotterdam, The Netherlands
Client: Municipality of Rotterdam
Program: single-pylon bridge with integrated parking garage and office building
Span: 931.75 ft.
Pylon height: 459.31 ft.
Design UNStudio: Ben van Berkel with Freek Loos, Hans Cromjongh and Ger Gijzen, Willemijn Lofvers, Sibo de Man, Gerard Nijenhuis, Manon Patinama, John Rebel, Ernst van Rijn, Hugo Schuurman, Caspar Smeets, Paul Toornend, Jan Willem Walraad, Dick Wetzels, Karel Vollers

Engineering: Ingenieursbureau Gemeentewerken Rotterdam, Rotterdam
Contractor steel works: Grootint, Dordrecht
Contractor concrete works: MBG/CFE, Brussels/Antwerp

1992–1994 Villa Wilbrink, Amersfoort, The Netherlands
Client: Mr. and Mrs. Wilbrink-van den Berg
Program: single-family house
Gross floor surface: 2,045 sq.ft.
Volume: 719 cu.yd.
Site: 1,927 sq.ft.
Design UNStudio: Ben van Berkel with Aad Krom and Jan van der Erven, Branimir Medic
Engineering: Bureau Bouwpartners, Hilversum

1993–1998 Möbius House, Het Gooi, The Netherlands
Client: anonymous
Program: single-family house
Gross floor surface: 5,579 sq.ft.
Volume: 2,943 cu.yd.
Site: 4.94 acres
Design UNStudio: Ben van Berkel with Aad Krom, Jen Alkema and Matthias Blass, Remco Bruggink, Marc Dijkman, Casper le Fèvre, Rob Hootsmans, Tycho Soffree, Giovanni Tedesco, Harm Wassink
Landscape architect: West 8, Rotterdam
Structural engineering: ABT, Velp

1995–1998 Bascule Bridge & Bridgemaster's House, Purmerend, The Netherlands
Client: Municipality of Purmerend
Gross floor surface: 969 sq.ft.
Volume: 392 cu.yd.

Design UNStudio: Ben van Berkel with Freek
Loos, Ger Gijzen and Sibo de Man, John Rebel,
Stefan Böwer, Stefan Lungmuss
Management and Engineering: IBA, Amsterdam

1995–1998 Het Valkhof Museum, Nijmegen, The Netherlands

Design UNStudio: Ben van Berkel with Henri Snel
(project co-ordination), Remco Bruggink, Rob
Hootsmans, Hugo Beschoor Plug, Walther Kloet,
Marc Dijkman, Jacco van Wengerden, Luc Veeger,
Florian Fischer, Carsten Kiselowsky
Landscape architect: Bureau B&B, Stedenbouw en
landschapsarchitectuur, Michael van Gessel; and
City of Nijmegen, Dept. of Urban Planning, Mark
van Gils
Interior: Ben van Berkel, Remco Bruggink
Exhibition: Studio Dumbar, Rotterdam in
collaboration with WAAC's, Rotterdam
Graphical Design: Total Design, Amsterdam
Project leading: Berns Projekt Management, Peter
Berns, Arnhem
Project management: Haskoning, Herman
Loonen, Nijmegen
Building director: Adviesbureau voor Bouwkosten
BV, ABKS, Bob Scholte, Arnhem
Constructor: Adviesbureau voor Bouwtechniek BV,
ABT, Gerard Doos, Arnhem
Cost management: Adviesbureau voor Bouw-
kosten BV, ABKS, Theo Schoenmakers, Arnhem
Advisor installation techniques: Ketel
Raadgevende Ingenieurs, Matthieu Mimpen, Delft
Lighting advisors: Hans Wolff & Partners, Hans
Wolff, Amsterdam
Construction contractor: Nelissen-van Egteren
Bouw Zuid BV, Venray

Facade construction: Blitta BV, Ton van der
Heyden, Venray
Mechanical installations: Stork installatietechniek,
Nijmegen
Electro technical installations: GTI Arnhem BV,
Arnhem
Elevator installations: Haushahn Möhringer Liften
BV, Haarlem
Ceiling: Verwol projectafbouw, Eric van der Veen,
Opmeer
Exterior ceiling: Berendsen-van Geemen BV,
Arnhem
Permanent and exhibition design: Karma design,
Paul and Fred van Gelderen, Breda
Supplier light installations: Zumtobel staff, Breda
Permanent interior: Merwede meubel & interieur,
Hardinxveld-Giessendam
Temporary interior: Kembo, Veenendaal
Soft furnishing: Theatex, Vinkeveen

1995–2000 Chapel, Hilversum, The Netherlands

Client: Regenboog Kerk, Hilversum
Program: church and social meeting center
Gross floor surface: 24,219 sq.ft.
Volume: 14,715 cu.yd.
Design UNStudio: Ben van Berkel with Harm
Wassink and Hans Sterck, Hjalmar Fredriksson,
Jacco van Wengerden

1997–2001 NMR Facility, Utrecht University, The Netherlands

Client: University of Utrecht
Program: laboratory for NMR Spectroscopy
Gross floor surface: 22,066 sq.ft.
Volume: 13,080 cu.yd.

Site: 5.19 acres
Design UNStudio: Ben van Berkel with Harm
Wassink, Ludo Grooteman, Walter Kloet, Mark
Westerhuis, Jacco van Wengerden, Aad Krom,
Paul Vriend, Marion Regitko, Jeroen Kreijnen,
Henri Snel, Laura Negrini, Remco Bruggink,
Marc Prins
Engineering: ABT, Amersfoort
Installations: BAM Techniques, Rotterdam

1996–2002 Electrical Substation, Innsbruck, Austria

Client: Innsbrucker Kommunalbetriebe AG
Program: 50/10 kV Substation
Gross floor surface: 27,104 sq.ft.
Volume: 11,772 cu.yd.
Site: 0.62 acres
Design UNStudio: Ben van Berkel with Hannes
Pfau, Jacco van Wengerden and Gianni Cito, Ludo
Grooteman, Laura Negrini, Casper le Fèvre, Eli
Aschkenasy, Hjalmar Frederikson, Hans Sterck,
Boudewijn Rosman, Yuri Werner
Engineering: Peter Ladurner-Rennau, Innsbruck
Building physics: Peter Fiby, Innsbruck

1998–2003 Prince Claus Bridge, Utrecht, The Netherlands

Client: Municipality of Utrecht
Program: single-pylon bridge
Pylon height: 299.87 ft.
Design UNStudio: Ben van Berkel with Freek
Loos, Ger Gijzen and Armin Hess, Suzanne Boyer,
Jeroen , Jacques van Wijk, Ludo Grooteman,
Henk Bultstra, Tobias Wallisser, Ron Roos
Management: DHV, Amersfoort
Engineering concrete foundations: DHV, Amersfoort

Engineering pylon and deck: Halcrow UK, London and Swindon

1999–2001 Water Villas, Almere, The Netherlands

Client: Visser Bouwmaatschappij BV, Huizen
Design: *UNStudio*: Ben van Berkel with Gianni Cito, Henri Snel, Boudewijn Rosman, Alexander Jung, Katrin Meyer, Aad Krom, Andreas Bogenschütz, Yuri Werner, KSK Tamura, Jasper Jägers, Stella Vesselinova, Martin Kuitert

1999–2004 La Defense Offices, Almere, The Netherlands

Client: Eurocommerce, Deventer
Design UNStudio: Ben van Berkel with Marco Hemmerling, Martin Kuitert, Henri Snel, Gianni Cito, Olaf Gisper, Yuri Werner, Marco van Helden, Eric Kauffman, Katrin Meyer, Tanja Koch, Igor Kebel, Marcel Buis, Ron Roos, Boudewijn Rosman, Stella Vesselinova

2000–2003 Living Tomorrow Pavilion, Amsterdam, The Netherlands

Client: Living Tomorrow, Vilvoorde
Program: showroom pavilion with House of the future and Office of the future.
Gross floor surface: 37,674 sq.ft.
Volume: 41,856 cu.yd.
Design UNStudio: Ben van Berkel with Igor Kebel, Aad Krom, Martin Kuitert, Markus Berger Ron Roos, Andreas Bogenschütz
Executive architect: Living Tomorrow, Vilvoorde

2000–2004 Hotel Castell, Zuoz, Switzerland

Client: Castell Zuoz AG, Herrliberg

Program: apartment building, hotel renovation and hammam
Gross floor surface: 59,202 sq.ft.
Apartment building: 32,292 sq.ft.
Parking building: 11,840 sq.ft.
Hotel kitchen: 4,306 sq.ft.
Hammam: 2,799 sq.ft.
Hotel rooms: 7,535 sq.ft.
Volume: 19,620 cu.yd.
Site: 0.54 acres
Design UNStudio: Ben van Berkel with Olaf Gipser and Pablo Rica, Sebastian Schaeffer, Andrew Benn, Dag Thies, Eric den Eerzamen, Ron Roos, Claudia Dorner, Martin Kuitert, Marco Hemmerling, Sophie Valla, Tina Bayerl, Peter Irmscher
Executive architect: Walter Dietsche AG, Chur
Advisors
Structural engineering: Edy Toscano AG, Pontresina
MEP engineering: Juerg Bulach AG, St. Moritz; Kaelin AG, St. Moritz; Giston AG, Samedan
Building physics: Kuster + Partner AG, Chur

2000–2006 VilLA NM, Upstate New York, USA

Client: anonymous
Program: single-family house
Gross floor surface: 2,691 sq.ft.
Volume: 915.60 cu.yd.
Site: 1.83 acres
Design UNStudio: Ben van Berkel with Olaf Gipser and Andrew Benn, Colette Parras, Jacco van Wengerden, Maria Eugenia Diaz, Jan Debelius, Martin Kuitert, Pablo Rica, Olga Vazquez-Ruano

Project consultant: Roemer Pierik, Rotterdam, The Netherlands
Construction: Henry and Quick Construction, Inc., Brooklyn, NY

2001–2006 Mercedes-Benz Museum, Stuttgart, Germany

Client: DaimlerChrysler Immobilien, Berlin
Project management: Drees & Sommer, Stuttgart
Gross floor surface: 376,737 sq.ft.
Volume: 353,160 cu.yd.
Site: 15.32 acres
Design UNStudio: Ben van Berkel, Tobias Wallisser, Caroline Bos with Marco Hemmerling, Hannes Pfau and Wouter de Jonge, Arjan Dingsté, Götz Peter Feldmann, Björn Rimner, Sebastian Schaeffer, Andreas Bogenschütz, Uli Horner, Ivonne Schickler, Dennis Ruarus, Erwin Horstmanshof, Derrick Diporedjo, Nanang Santoso, Robert Brixner, Alexander Jung, Matthew Johnston, Rombout Loman, Arjan van der Bliek, Fabian Evers, Nuno Almeida, Ger Gijzen, Tjago Nunes, Boudewijn Rosman, Ergian Alberg, Gregor Kahlau, Mike Herud, Thomas Klein, Simon Streit, Taehoon Oh, Jenny Weiss, Philipp Dury, Carin Lamm, Anna Carlquist, Jan Debelius, Daniel Kalani, Evert Klinkenberg
Realization: UNStudio with Wenzel + Wenzel, Stuttgart; Matias Wenzel with Markus Schwarz, Clemens Schulte-Mattler, Ina Karbon
Team: Nicola Kühnle, Florian Erhard, Michael Fischinger, Christoph Friedrich, Peter Holzer, Christoph Krinn, Stefan Linder, Simon Schneider, Walter Ulrich, Gabriele Völker, Katrin Widmann, Christina Brecher, Stefanie Hertwerck, Ingolf Gössel, Ulla Ittensohn, Volker Hilpert, Thomas

Koch, Ulrike Kolb, Bendix Pallesen-Mustikay, Marc Schwesinger and Thuy Duong Du, Kathrin Steimle, Florian Goscheff, Thomas Hertlein, Yvonne Galdys, Deniz Hocaoglu, Katerina Karapanceva, Anka Volk, Patrick Yong
Exhibition concept and design: HG Merz, Stuttgart
Interior: UN Studio with Concrete Architectural Associates, Amsterdam
Curtain design: Inside Outside - Petra Blaisse, Amsterdam
Structure: Werner Sobek Ingenieure, Stuttgart
Geometry: Arnold Walz, Stuttgart
Climate engineering: Transsolar Energietechnik, Stuttgart
Cost estimation: Nanna Fütterer, Stuttgart/Berlin
Infrastructure: David Johnston, Arup, London
Landscaping: Knoll Ökoplan GmbH, Sindelfingen

2002–2007 Agora Theater, Lelystad, The Netherlands
Client: Municipality of Lelystad
Program: theater with two halls and a multi-functional space, restaurant and bar
Gross floor surface: 75,347 sq.ft.
Volume: 39,239 cu.yd.
Site: 0.72 acres
Design UNStudio: Ben van Berkel with Gerard Loozekoot, Jacques van Wijk and Job Mouwen, Holger Hoffmann, Khoi Tran, Christian Veddeler, Christian Bergmann, Sabine Habicht, Ramon Hernandez, Ron Roos, René Wysk, Claudia Dorner, Markus Berger, Markus Jacobi, Ken Okonkwo, Jorgen Grahl-Madsen
Executive architect: B+M, Den Haag
Theater technique: Prinssen en Bus Raadgevende

Ingenieurs, Uden
Engineering: Pieters Bouwtechniek, Almere
Acoustics/Fire strategy: DGMR, Arnhem

2003–2004 Galleria Department Store, Seoul, South Korea
Client: HANWHA STORES CO., LTD
Design UNStudio: Ben van Berkel and Caroline Bos with Astrid Piber, Ger Gijzen, Cristina Bolis, Markus Hudert, Colette Parras, Arjan van der Bliek, Christian Veddeler, Albert Gnodde, Richard Crofts, Barry Munster, Mafalda Bottelo, Elke Uitz, Harm Wassink
Structural engineers: Arup & Partners, Arjan Habraken, Amsterdam (schematic design)
Lighting design: Arup Lighting, Rogier van der Heide, IALD, Seoul (schematic design and design development)
Wayfinding design: Bureau Mijksenaar, Martijn Geerdes, Amsterdam (design development)
Façade design: RAC – Rah Architecture Consulting, Seoul
Interior design: Kesson International, Seoul
Façade construction: Dongshin C G E Co. Ltd, Dongshin Glass Co. Ltd., Seoul
Façade lighting: Xilver BV, Seoul
Interior construction: Hanwha Engineering & Construction Corp., Seoul
Façade construction: Hanwha Engineering & Construction Corp., Seoul

2004–2006 Tea House on Bunker, Vreeland, The Netherlands
Gross floor surface: 861 sq.ft.
Site: 581 sq.ft.
Volume: 589 cu.yd.
Client: Cor van Zadelhoff
Design UNStudio: Ben van Berkel, Gerard Loozekoot with René Wysk, Job Mouwen and Marcel Buis, Thomas de Vries, Holger Hoffmann, Eric den Eerzamen, Joakim Kaminsky, Peter Irmscher, Daniel Kalani, Anika Voigt, Eric Coppolse, Stephan Albrecht
Project management: Rietmeyer Huisvestingsadviseurs, Ronald Cos, Geert Wilmink, Almere
Constructor: ABT, Rob Nijsse, Velp
Construction: ABT, Rob Nijsse, Stephan Toonen, Velp
Equipment: ABT, Onno Janse, Velp
Building physics: ABT, Mark van Veghel, Velp
Exterior lighting: Arup lighting, Amsterdam; Rogier van der Heide, Marion Tränkle
Façade: Sorba, Winterswijk
Glass: Metaglas, Tiel
Sliding door: Hallington, Vianen
Interior structure: Van Schaik, Breukelen
Interieur completion: Benschop, Zoetermeer
Floor: Van Zoelen, Badhoevedorp
Electrical equipment: Bart Lodder, Breukelen
Water equipment: Engeltherm, Montfoort
Sanitary equipment: Smit installatietechniek, Utrecht

Note: The dates cited are those on which planning began and not when the buildings were completed.

1989
Kunst & Bedrijf, office interior, Amsterdam, The Netherlands

1990
Villa Härtel, villa renovation and transformation into grand café/restaurant, Amersfoort, The Netherlands
Schellerhoek, 129 single family houses, Zwolle, The Netherlands

1991
De Kolk, housing, hotel, offices, shopping mall, parking, Amsterdam, The Netherlands

1992
Rijksmuseum Twenthe, Enschede, The Netherlands
Multifunctional center Kattenbroek, Amersfoort, The Netherlands
De Kolk, housing, hotel, offices, shopping mall, parking, Amsterdam, The Netherlands
ACOM, renovation office building, Amersfoort, The Netherlands
Piet Hein-tunnel, tunnel and two service buildings, Amsterdam, The Netherlands

1993
Interior director's room NAi, Rotterdam, The Netherlands
Housing Rijkerswoerd, Arnhem, The Netherlands
Coffee cup Alessi
Window Construmat Product design, Spain
Street furniture Willemsplein, Rotterdam, The Netherlands
Parking Erasmus Bridge, Rotterdam, The Netherlands

1994
Shopping center renovation, Emmen, The Netherlands
Diaconessen area, 50 apartments, Arnhem, The Netherlands
Villa De Lange, Sukatani, Indonesia

1995
De rubbermat, transformation industrial complex Unilever, Rotterdam, Study/group exhibition, The Netherlands
Rijkerswoerd 2, 20 single-family houses, Arnhem, The Netherlands
Housing Sporenburg, Amsterdam, The Netherlands
Wilhelminakade, 44 apartments, Groningen, The Netherlands
Pedestrian Bridge, Amsterdam, The Netherlands

1996
Supermarket and parking, Emmen, The Netherlands
City hall and theater, IJsselstein, The Netherlands
Exhibition design at Royal Palace, Amsterdam, The Netherlands
Arnhem Central Station, Arnhem, The Netherlands
De Aker, 3 housing blocks, Amsterdam, The Netherlands
28 single-family houses, Seizoenenbuurt, Amersfoort, The Netherlands
Supermarket and 56 apartments and parking, Emmen, The Netherlands
"De Blauwe Grift," apartment building, Utrecht, The Netherlands
Key area, 129 single-family apartments and 31 apartments, Nijmegen, The Netherlands
Masterplan Arnhem Central, Arnhem, The Netherlands
De rubbermat, transformation industrial complex Unilever, Rotterdam, Study/Waste disposal, Schieweg, Delft, The Netherlands

1997
Supermarket and 56 apartments and parking, Emmen, The Netherlands

1998
La Tour, office tower, Apeldoorn, The Netherlands

1999
De Loswal, apartment building with 40 single-family houses, Amsterdam, The Netherlands
La Residence, offices, Nieuwegein, The Netherlands
Infrastructural interventions, overpass and sound screens A2, 's-Hertogenbosch, The Netherlands

2000
Park and Rijn, office towers, Arnhem, The Netherlands
Exhibition layout Envisioning Architects Schirn Kunsthalle, Frankfurt, Germany
Exhibition layout NEO Centraal Museum, Utrecht, The Netherlands

2001
Jewish Historical Museum, extension and renovation Amsterdam, The Netherlands
Hotel Castell, apartments, hotel renovation and hammam, Zuoz, The Netherlands

2002
SUM, table, Gispen, The Netherlands
Infrastructural interventions, overpass/sound screen, Everdingen-Deil and Zaltbommel Empel, The Netherlands
Infrastructural interventions A2, Eindhoven, The Netherlands

2003
Research laboratory University Groningen, Groningen, The Netherlands
Chair design for Fritz Hansen, Design
Exhibition design "Summer of Love Schirn" Kunsthalle, Frankfurt, Germany
Exhibition "Evolution of Space," Barcelona, Spain
Sofa Circle, Walter Knoll, Zetel, Germany
Switch Tray, Alessi, Design
Tea and Coffee Towers, Alessi

2005
Exhibition design "Kurt Schwitters," Boijmans van Beuningen Museum, Rotterdam, The Netherlands

2006
Exhibition design "Evolution of Space," Yale Gallery, New Haven, Connecticut, USA